*More inside information
from those
precocious pranksters,
Eggbert and Eggberta*

Here's an all-new collection of the wit, wisdom, and hilarious antics of two of the most winsome little characters who never walked the earth. While they wait to make their entrance, Eggbert and Eggberta treat us to their unique views on the outside world— a prenatal prognosis that will give birth to endless chuckles.

Books by LAF

Eggbert: Belly Laughs
Eggbert Easy Over
Eggbert: Funny Side Up
Scrambled Eggbert
Strictly Fresh Eggbert

Published by POCKET BOOKS

EGGBERT: Belly Laughs

Cartoons by LAF

P A KANGAROO BOOK

PUBLISHED BY POCKET BOOKS NEW YORK

EGGBERT: Belly Laughs

POCKET BOOK edition published February, 1974

3rd printing....................September, 1977

This original POCKET BOOK edition is printed from brand-new
plates made from newly set, clear, easy-to-read type.
POCKET BOOK editions are published by
POCKET BOOKS,
a Simon & Schuster Division of
GULF & WESTERN CORPORATION
1230 Avenue of the Americas,
New York, N.Y. 10020.
Trademarks registered in the United States
and other countries.

3487

EGGBERT:
Belly Laughs

"NEXT TIME I'M MOVING INTO
A FURNISHED PLACE!"

" CHICKEN LITTLE WAS <u>RIGHT!</u>"

" DO YOU THINK WE ORTA CALL
FOR RESERVATIONS ?"

"SHOULD I MOVE, OR JUST
WAIT 'TIL I'M EVICTED?"

"QUOTING MOM, 'THIS IS ONE OF OUR <u>YUK</u> DAYS!'"

" WOULD YA BELIEVE
RADIANT HEAT ? "

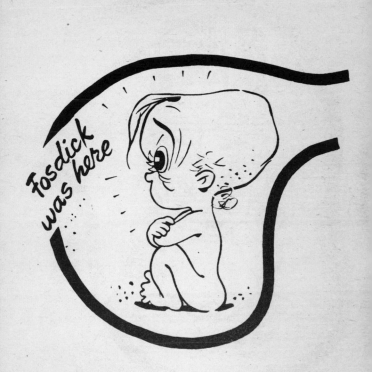

"WHAT 'CHA KNOW...I'M A RE-RUN!"

"LET ME MAKE THIS
CRYSTAL-CLEAR...!"

LISTEN TO THE ACTION WHEN
I YELL, "<u>FORE!</u>"

" ONE LUMP OR TWO ?"

"WHEN I SNEEZE... SHE BURPS!
FAR OUT, MAN... FAR OUT!"

" <u>SHE</u> THINKS SHE'S GOT
A BACKACHE ! "

"THEN AGAIN, MAYBE I SHOULDN'T..."

"DON'T CALL ME...I'LL CALL YOU!"

" IT'S AN INVITATION TO A
COMING-OUT PARTY!"

"I'D GET A BETTER PICTURE
IF I HAD AN OUTSIDE AERIAL!"

"IF HE HAD A BEARD I'D CALL HIM RIP VAN WINKLE!"

" IT'S FOR YOU! "

"MUST BE A BETTER MAIDEN
SPEECH THAN 'WAH-H-H'!"

"ZEESH! SHE'S COMING UP
WITH ANOTHER BELLY LAUGH!"

"EVER WONDER WHERE
CLAUSTROPHOBIA GOT ITS START?"

" AT LEAST THE UTILITIES
ARE INCLUDED ! "

" PARDNER,
THIS PLACE AIN'T BIG ENOUGH
FOR THE TWO OF US! "

" OKEH, IF <u>WE</u> INHALE WHEN <u>SHE</u> DOES,
WE'LL GET HER INTO HER GIRDLE ! "

"ANOTHER FAT ARGUMENT
ABOUT MY NAME!"

"WONDER IF THEY'LL THINK
I'M CUTE ?"

" SO, MAYBE YOU'D PREFER JUMPING ? "

" THEY'VE JUST NOW FIGURED THE
PROBABILITY OF TWINS! "

" HERE'S ONE! LARGE SUNNY ROOM,
KIDS ALLOWED... "

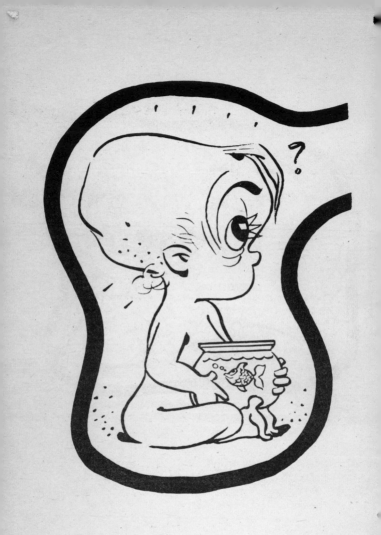

"MAYBE I BETTER HAND
HERMAN OUT FIRST..."

" WONDER IF DOC WILL TAKE
A LITTLE COACHING...?"

"LAST TIME I KICK _THAT_ BIG LUNK!"

" DAMN IT... STOP ROLLING OVER
ON _MY_ SIDE! "

"DEAR DIARY: JUST ONE MORE WEEK BEFORE I MEET MOM!"

"EXIT STAGE LEFT!"

"THAT'S NOT QUITE WHAT THEY MEAN WHEN THEY SAY WE'RE AN ACCIDENT!"

"WHO SAYS EVERYTHING STOPS
IN A POWER BLACKOUT?"

"FROM THE WAY MOM TALKS,
I'D HAVE MORE ROOM IN <u>POP</u>! "

" WHAT A CHISELER! CLAIMING ME
AS A <u>DEPENDENT</u> ! "

" THE PLANNING COMMISSION
THAT DESIGNED THIS JOINT
WERE KNUCKLE-HEADS!"

"COME OFF IT, KID! OUR GENES
MIGHT GO 'BOOM' AND GUM
UP THE WORKS!"

"HEY, POP...IF GEORGE WASHINGTON IS THE FATHER OF OUR COUNTRY..."

" RUMMM...VUMMM...VUMMM...
JUST DOWN HERE FOR A PIT STOP!"

"ZEESH! HER THERMOSTAT IS COMPLETELY OUT OF WHACK!"

" ... AND IN THIS CORNER, THE
WELTER-WEIGHT KICKING CHAMP
OF THE WORLD ! "

"QUIT STALLING
WITH THE 'HO-HO'S' POP,
AND GIVE WITH THE PRESENTS!"

"EARTHQUAKE, HELL! MOM JUST ATE
ANOTHER TACO!"

" I'LL JUST KEEP SENDING 'EM BACK
UNTIL SHE LEARNS I DON'T LIKE
POACHED EGGS! "

"...AND NOW FOR THE
HIGH HURDLE EVENT..."

"WHO'S NERVOUS? POP ALWAYS
USES MOM'S HAIRSPRAY
FOR A DEODORANT!"

" THE OLD MAN NEVER LEARNS
TO PUT THE SLIDES IN
RIGHT-SIDE UP ! "

"RE-DEEP, RE-DEEP! THAT OUGHT
TO SHAKE 'EM UP!"

" MOM SURE PICKED A HELL-OF-A-TIME
TO START DEEP-KNEE BENDS! "

"LAY OFF! YOU KNOW I'VE GOT
A DUST ALLERGY!"

" HEY MOM! GUESS WHAT? YOU
MUSTA SWALLOWED A POT SEED!"

"WHAT A DAME! IN THE DEAD OF
WINTER SHE GOES APE ON
POPSICLES!"

"LOOKS LIKE
YOU SPLIT A SEAM, KIDDO!"

"OKEH, MOM...
READY FOR THE FIRST COURSE!"

"SO, I'M CAUTIOUS.
MAKE SOMETHING OF IT!"

"SO I JUST HAPPEN TO COME
WITH MORE OPTIONAL EQUIPMENT,
THAT'S ALL!"

"MOM JUST BLEW
ANOTHER FUSE AT POP!"

"HOW IN HELL DO WE GET HER
TO CUT DOWN ON THE BUBBLE-BATH?"

"OH, WOW! IT MUST HAVE BEEN THAT LAST 'HARVEY WALL BANGER' POP MIXED LAST NIGHT!!!"

" MAYBE I OUGHTA MAKE A
LIST OF DO'S AND DON'TS
FOR THE NEXT TENANTS !! "

"NO WONDER THERE'S TWO OF US...
THE WAY OUR OLD MAN STAMMERS!"

" THE WAY HER OLD LADY GIVES ADVICE,
YOU'D THINK MEDICAL ADVANCEMENT
STOPPED AFTER HER PREGNANCY. "

" SOMEHOW I GATHER GRANDMA
DOESN'T APPROVE OF MY BEING HERE!"

" AS I GET IT,
THEY MET ON A PROTEST MARCH! "

" MOM, THAT'S NO WAY TO TALK ABOUT MY POP! "

" PUT 'EM BACK!
WANNA GET MOM ARRESTED? "

"YOIKS! MY VOICE IS CHANGING!"

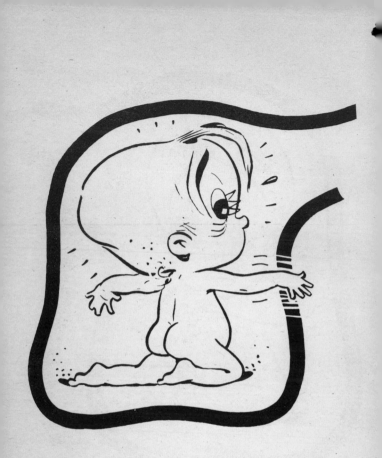

"THIS HIGH-WIRE ACT OF HER'S
HAS GOTTA GO!"

" I SURE AIN'T WORTH A DAMN
UNTIL SHE'S HAD HER
FIRST CUP OF COFFEE! "

"GAWDAMIT, POP...
DROP THE OTHER SHOE!"

" SHE SAYS FOR US TO COOL IT
A FEW DAYS MORE... MATERNITY
WARD'S FULL UP! "

" TOMORROW'S MY BIRTHDAY ! "

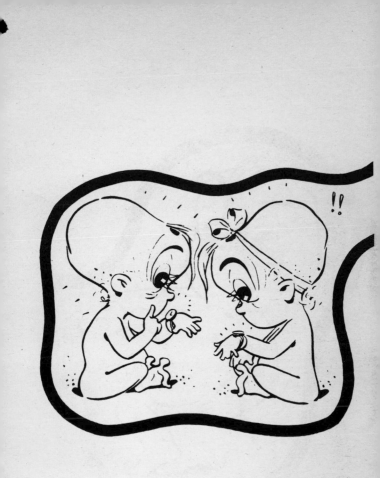

"STEADY...
SYNCHRONIZE WATCHES... _NOW!_"

" ONE SMALL STEP FOR MAN..."

"SHE'S GOTTA BE KIDDIN'! ON OUR
WAY TO THE HOSPITAL SHE GETS
A YEN FOR A <u>PIZZA</u>!"

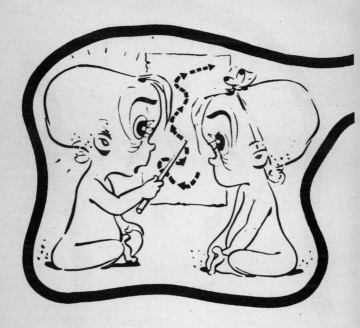

" NOW REMEMBER.
JUST FOLLOW THIS MAP
AND YOU'RE HOME FREE ! "

" LOOK, WE'RE JUST MOVING TOPSIDE...
NOT TAKING A WORLD TOUR ! "

" BAD TIMING, KID.
THIS IS DOC'S GOLF DAY ! "

" RELAX! THE ELEVATOR'S STUCK! "

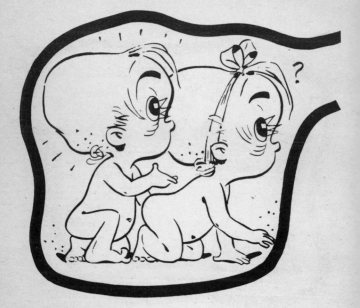

"WOMEN AND CHILDREN FIRST!"

"... A DETOUR SIGN?"

"SURE HOPE DOC'S GOT STEADY HANDS!"

" THIS IS A HELLUVA TIME TO BE
CHECKING YOUR MEDICAL BOOK!"

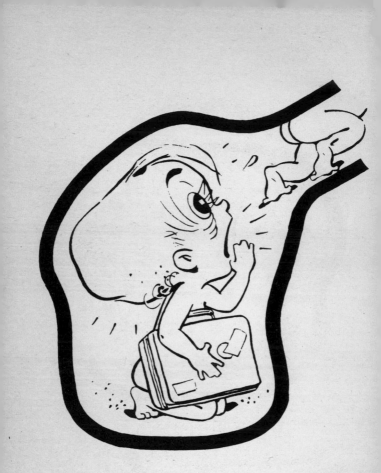

"HEY! KEEP THE HATCH OPEN!
MORE COMIN'!"

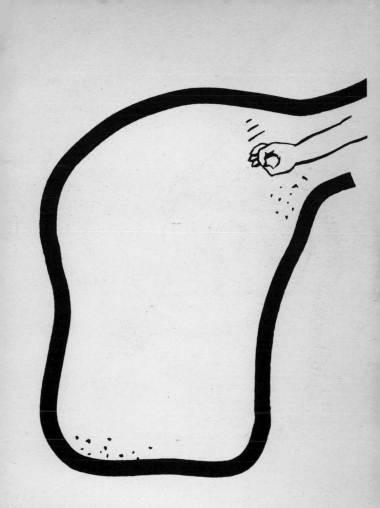

"EVERYTHING'S A-OK, FOLKS!"

"THIS IS A HELL OF A WAY
TO SPEND A SATURDAY AFTERNOON!"